REJECTED FOR PURPOSE

CHRISTINA NEPTUNE

(REJECTED FOR PURPOSE)
Copyright © 2009 by Christina Neptune

ISBN: 978-1-63877-371-9

TABLE OF CONTENTS

INTRODUCTION

R ejection is a time of isolation. It is a painful process, but it is necessary. Being isolated from rejection brings forth purpose that was dormant within you. During the pain, the objective isn't revealed. Rejection conceives purpose. Webster's dictionary defines **purpose** as "a reason for which something is done or created for which something exists." In Hebrew, the word **rejection** is defined as "postponement, disqualification, carving, sculpturing, neglect, abandonment, and omission." When dissecting the word rejection, the prefix "re" means, again and back. The suffix ejection is the act of expelling or forcing out. We can also define rejection as dismissing or refusing a proposal or an idea. Biblically, it is described in I Samuel 8:7 - "For they are rejecting me, not you." When you walk with God, you become a target. God reveals that when we decide to walk in our purpose instead of His, rejection often forces us to align to in His perfect will.

I went through a miscarriage, abandonment, and heartbreak, which birthed this book. I went through a period of isolation that allowed me to embrace my gifting. The goal of this book is to capture the many forms of rejection. There are different stages of rejection and healing phases of rejection. The most common form of rejection is social rejection; it usually occurs when somebody is excluded from a social relationship or an interaction, which led to disturbing consequences. I've had my share of social rejection; I've been wounded from bullying as a child and endured violent relationships.

When we understand that rejection is part God's plan to place us where we need to be, we will realize it is not punishment. It is a time to hear God's voice clearly and move in obedience without the chaos and loud voices around you. It is at that moment you can be cultivated and matured.

This book will birth what God is trying to expel out of you. It will give you a more in-depth understanding of why we all go through seasons of isolation. I will discuss critical characters in the bible that have endured rejection. We will explore the different types of rejections that Leah, King David, Joseph, Jesus, and I have suffered. It will further explain why rejection creates purpose.

Rejected by man, favored by God: My Joseph Season

The story of Joseph has always been one of my favorites. Joseph was the son of Jacob and Rachel. In Genesis, chapter 37, Joseph was sold into slavery by his brothers. There are so many ways I can relate to Joseph. Joseph went through a season of imprisonment and being wrongfully accused of things he didn't do. In the end, it actually turned out for his good. Joseph spent many years in suffering, and his father even grieved, thinking that he'd lost his son. Joseph was shown favor because of his gifts. The ability to interpret dreams delivered him from imprisonment. Favor became his portion, and his gifts made room for him.

Joseph remained in the Lord, and God made sure that whatever he did was successful. I saw a lot of that in me. There were many times I compared our stories and saw so many similarities. If any of you have read the story of Joseph, it is gut-wrenching... The trials and tribulations that he went through were very sacrificial. What destroyed him was used to save his family.

As a little girl, I always felt different and set apart from my siblings. At the age of 6, I repeatedly had dreams of who I would be and what I would become. As a child, I always had visions of being someone of high importance. Although I never knew how it would happen, I just knew God would show out in my life. The early years of my life were great and not so great. My father and mother were immigrants from Haiti. There is nearly a 20 year age difference between the two. I had the luxury of living a lifestyle with a silver spoon in my mouth and living where I had to struggle.

My story is very similar to Joseph's. I've always felt as if I was less significant than the rest of my dad's children. I always felt as if I had to compete to show that I was worthy. In the early years of my life, a lot of brothers and sisters surrounded me. Nevertheless, while being surrounded by so many siblings, I always remember feeling the love from my father. Whenever I was in my father's presence, I always felt as if I was the only child in the room. The way my father used to love and hug me was symbolic of how my heavenly father loved me. I remember being with my father everywhere that he went. I remember him being so proud of me and showing me off amongst his friends and people that knew him in the community. My father was a very well-known entrepreneur in the Little Haiti community. Whenever they saw him, I would be me on his right side. My brother and I were always present with my father in his daily business dealings.

I had the luxury of attending the finest private schools. I even experience eating at the finest restaurants from Fountain Blue, and the list goes on. But one day, all of that changed. I remember tension between my mother and my father. My parents weren't together no did they reside in the same residence. My younger brother resided with my mother and I resided with my father briefly. Between the grades of Kindergarten and First grade.

One day, I was at school and HRS (Health and Rehabilative Services), which is now DCF (Department of Children and Family Services), came to the school with my mom to get me.

That is when my whole life changed. The lifestyle that I was accustomed to living would change as well. I was placed back in my mother's custody; we lived in homeless shelters and at different people's houses. There were days at a time when I wouldn't see my mother because there wasn't room for her to be at the homes she temporarily placed us in. They would only accept my younger brother and me. My younger brother and I shared the same mother and same father. My mother was the only one who conceived more than one child from my father.

In the process of transitioning, I remember all the things that my mother endured. I went from navigating back and forth from a two-story house with a pool and a jacuzzi and my mother's reasonably nice home to now living in a homeless shelter. It was extremely tough for me as a seven-year-old. I've experienced sharing rooms with other large-sized families. I've watched my mom going from having a car to having no car, and struggling. But through those times, I remained humble. I don't remember ever complaining or asking God why. I remember crying for my father a lot, and my mother making me feel horrible for missing my dad.

Even though I didn't understand what was getting ready to occur, this was the beginning of greatness being birthed in me. I watched my mother struggle for quite some time, eventually we relocated to Kissimmee, Florida in the late 80s. Kissimmee is a small town located less than 10 minutes away from Orlando, Florida. My mom relocated and found a new job. She went to work without a car, and I watched her work, walking miles a day. I couldn't even begin to fathom the sacrifice and struggle she endured to attend to us.

My mother was unable to afford a babysitter. So as a child, I grew up way before time permitted. My brother and I stayed home alone as my mom worked double shifts, and there were so many days that we didn't get to see her. She would see us when we were sleeping. Every day, my mother would give reminders to not answer the door for anyone, and if they were to come into the apartment for inspection, we would have to find a hiding place in hopes of not being discovered and separated from our mother. My brother and I had a particular area where we would always go. It was a sleeper sofa, and we would hide under there until everything was clear. We didn't have many toys, and the many toys that we had were hand me downs. But my brother and I were extremely creative. We created our dolls with college ruled paper, and we used Crayola markers and crayons to design how we wanted them to look; we created our happiness.

We were now in a new area, getting ready to start a new school, and it was tough. My brother and I endured a lot of bullying. Not to mention a lot of verbal abuse and rejection from many of the kids in school. We didn't dress like the other kids in the Nike and Cross Color clothing. We wore shelter hand me downs. My mom just couldn't afford those things. Whenever our pants got to our ankles, my mom would just cut them into shorts. She would make a way with what we had available.

Even though my mother did her best, the kids and peers around us didn't understand, and their words began to break me. I spent most of my childhood tormented; I was set apart. Chosen, but confused about my destiny because of how people treated me. I was so sad that the children didn't have any filter at that time. The choice words that they use to describe who they thought I was painful. It almost made me forget who God said that I was. The bullying that I endured forced me to try and be something that I wasn't. I tried to blend in with the crowd, but no matter how much I tried to blend in, I still endured the bullying.

There was a part of me that wanted to feel the presence and warmth of my dad. We had been separated for quite some time since relocating to Central Florida. Approximately 2 years later, my brother and I were given the opportunity to visit my dad for the summer. The summers were amazing. It allowed me to forget the suffering that we endured. It also made me forget the struggles that we had to go through. For once, I was able to be a child. The memories of coming to my dad's house for the summer are amazing. Imagine visiting and being able to jump into the warm pool and jacuzzi, and getting the most up-to-date clothing. It gave me time to be around my siblings I was once connected to. But one summer, things changed.

I had an older sibling who lived up North. My dad would fly him down, so he could spend the summers with us. One summer, he was involved in a serious accident that nearly took his life. My brother was hit by a reckless driver while riding his bicycle. The accident caused physical damage to his body. I was always happy to see this particular brother. We had a connection since I was a child. There was a huge age difference, but as a young girl, you desire the protection of your big brother. One day, this changed for me.

One summer evening, I remember being in my room watching TV. My big brother placed his hands between my legs and touched my private area. He had to have been at least 16 to 18 years old. I don't remember his exact age. I didn't understand what was going on. I knew it wasn't right. As the summer came to an end, I went back home. My big brother would send letters that my mom intercepted. My mom was very alarmed, and she suspected that something had taken place, that he had touched me. I remember denying it several times, acting like nothing ever happened. The letter my mom intercepted gave graphic sexual details of what he would do to my mom and he had drawn a picture of his penis.

After that summer, I was never the same. I was 11 going on 12, then. I was getting ready to start middle school, and that was the coming of age. This is when things started changing. I became vicious in school. I was trying so hard to be like the others who tormented me throughout my childhood. Being somebody else made me forget what happened. I was still trying to make sense of everything.

As time went by, things kind of took a toll for the worse. During my teenage years, I was heavily into drugs. I took sleeping pills, ecstasy, marijuana and a whole list of other drugs. It was easy for me to do these things because my mom still maintained the same demanding work schedule she had since we relocated. She worked days and nights. We barely saw her. I became heavily promiscuous. I was having sexual encounters with men twice my age. The sex became therapy. Eventually, it became too much for my mother and she sent me away to live with my father. I was so angry with my mom for sending me away, but it was part of the assignment. It was part of the plan God had for me. It was part of the purpose that God designed for my life.

Immediately when I moved in with my dad, he embraced me. I now had my own room. I didn't have to share it with my little brother. I was now in a place that brought me joy as a child, but also held some painful memories. I was now sleeping in a room that haunted me of the memories of molestation I tried to bury - the same memories that have kept me in bondage and imprisoned. I no longer felt protected and safe.

The same habits I created while living with my mother transferred when I moved back home to Miami with my father. The only difference was I was smoking marijuana and drinking. The pill-popping stopped, but the promiscuity continued. The attention I didn't get in Central Florida met me in Miami. It was the wrong attention. I had a longing to be needed, wanted, and loved. The moment I received some kind of attention, it made me feel like I was somebody. It caused me to lessen my morals, my character, and my values. I used it as a coping mechanism for what I couldn't express.

My mom rejected me. I was separated from my baby brother, who I was connected to for so long. My mom broke our bond and I resented her for that. Conveying my feelings turned into a form of rebellion. My life was headed in a downward spiral. I had a younger sister who despised me and made it clear on all levels. I was sneaking out of my dad's house and going to parties to avoid the hurt of not being accepted. One party that I snuck out for led to me being raped my senior year of high school. Now, I had another issue I was trying to deal with. It took a toll even more on my behavior. School wasn't even important anymore. I only showed up to school to smoke and drink because it was impossible to do so in my dad's household. Drugs and alcohol were frowned upon. Eventually, my dad became fed-up with my behavior. Imagine being raped one night and sneaking home the next morning to your dad realizing you hadn't been home... only to receive the news that you're getting kicked out. Rejection strikes again.

My mother didn't want me. Now, my dad didn't want me. I recall packing up my things and my dad calling a taxicab to transport us to the airport. I cried and pleaded with my dad for another chance. He walked away as if I meant nothing to him.

I was faced with two options, return to my mother, where I was faced with more rejection or remain in Miami and make the best of it. I refunded my plane ticket and stayed in Miami. I stayed with some friends from high school and took on a job as an exotic dancer. This was the quickest job I could get and the fastest quickest way I could make money. Here I was, again, getting the wrong kind of attention making money.

While all of this was going on, there was tension between the high school friend I was staying with, which led to a physical altercation and left me homeless. Your senior year of high school is supposed to be one of the most memorable moments of your life. I missed senior brunches, homecomings, trips, and even prom. I was just trying to survive.

I didn't stay homeless for too long. The same acquaintance that brought my classmate and I into the club offered me a place to stay. She was a single mom with two children toddler children. I had to make a pallet on the floor to sleep. Her best friend also lived in the apartment with her boyfriend. They slept on the living room floor. Jealousy started to surface. Not only was the best friend's boyfriend making passes at me, but I was accused of being the one making the advances. There I was, trying to explain this wasn't who I was. The tension between me and acquaintance that offered a roof over my head started to surface because all the men she was interested in were interested in me. You know what they say about jealousy - it's an ugly disease and it will cause you to do things that are painful.

Working at the strip club didn't last long for me. I was juggling high school and working nights at the club. I knew I needed a change of scenery and employment. I landed a job at the local Burger King, located by my high school. I was receiving unwanted attention again. Restaurant managers were making advances and insinuating that I was the one who asked for it.

During the time I was working at Burger King, I had become acquainted with a gentleman in Publix. We were casually dating. He knew a lot of the troubles I was enduring. He was aware of my living arrangements. He became a way of escape. Escape from the advances at the apartment, escape from the disrespect I was receiving from the young lady who rented the apartment. He was picking me up and taking me to school. We both needed companionship. His fiancé had just died, and I was dying on the inside. It felt so good to be wanted. It was temporary, but it filled that void in my life. My dad didn't want anything to do with me. I was still hurt by my mom. Little did I know, I was getting ready to face another dilemma.

I was expecting to return to the same apartment where I had been residing in my senior year. When I returned, it was empty. It was empty, just like my spirit. Everyone in the apartment had vacated without any warning. There I was, standing in an empty apartment. No lights. No food. No water. I had nowhere to go. I called the only person I knew I could count on - the gentleman that I received companionship from. I didn't notify him immediately. After being without food and water, I remember getting really sick and feverish. He came to my aid and rescue. I resided with him and his best friend for quite some time. The transition was rocky, but it beat being without food and water. I was just dealing with seasons of rejection. I wasn't able to heal from each of the situations. I just carried the weight of everything on my shoulders. But through it all, I continued to believe in God and rest in His promises. I knew the things that were occurring in my life were not my portion, but they were a part of the process.

Some time went by. The very man that I sought companionship from, him and I parted ways. It was amicable. I found myself not wanting to be alone more often than usual. I tried reconnecting to people who didn't value me because the rejection cut so deep. I was hopping from house to house, being violent and violated by men on a daily basis. There were times I would find myself sleeping and wake up to men trying to take advantage of me because I was in a vulnerable situation and I had nowhere to go. Every time I was violated, I would find somewhere else to go, only to deal with the same situation that I dealt with in the past. I remember being so depressed and so suicidal. I was hopeful that my situation would change.

One day, I met this guy named G at a convenient store. I walked to the store to get a pach of cigarettes. Within days he took me into his home and helped me get my life back in order. He introduced me to his family, and he embraced me. It finally felt like I found the person of my dreams. During this connection, I decided to move back in with my mom in Central Florida. The feelings of resentment were still there, but I tried to make the best of it. I was only there to kill time. I had put in an application to attend Homestead Job Corps just so I can be closer to G. While waiting for Job Corps to give me the call to attend their campus, I would visit G. I was doing all the extra stuff a young girl would do so prove her love. I was20 years old and head over heels in love.

Infidelity began to rear its ugly head in my relationship with G. I recollect doing his laundry one day and making sure the pockets were empty before I placed his pants in the washer. I found a heap of phone numbers in his pocket. The devastation was so real. While I was away, there wasn't a doubt in my mind that infidelity was taking place. I was witnessing it with my own eyes. I knew G was being unfaithful. The distance between us revealed who he really was when given the opportunity. I confronted G and we broke up. I eventually took him back, and months later, he proposed. The engagement ring he gave me turned my finger green! The value of that ring showed the value of our relationship. It was flawed and fake. The engagement ring was a reflection of how G truly felt about me and my existence.

I didn't understand it at the time, but I was being set up for rejection so that I could seek God. Isaiah 55:6 verse says, "Seek the Lord while he may be found call upon him while he is near. " I was in a season where I wanted everything I desired. I would even have conversations with God, telling him when I fulfill everything I want in my life that I would do His will.

This was the motto I lived by for years. At the time, seeking man's love was more important than seeking the love of God. I had become restless with being rejected. I knew God was drawing me closer to Him, although I had countless run-ins with law enforcement and had been placed in jail several times. Not to mention the countless number of miscarriages and ectopic pregnancies. I still was trying to do things my way. I thought my desires were greater than the Lord's. It says in His words in Isaiah 55:8-9, "For my thoughts are not your thoughts, neither are your ways my ways, declares the Lord. As the heavens are higher than the earth, so are my ways higher than your ways, and my thoughts than your thoughts."

There was a purpose for it all. The purpose had everything to do with what was getting ready to take place in my life. It was for the Glory of God. The pain and suffering I had encountered through the years were getting ready to birth something miraculous. Even after all the trials and tribulations, I still believed. The type of people that were in my life did not reflect what God had for me. It showed the exact opposite of God's promises. It was like the meme I saw on social media with the young child not wanting to give up the small teddy bear because he could not see God had a bigger teddy bear behind His back. This is what I was going through. I thought I was receiving God's best, but I was not. He had better for me, but I was delaying it with my desires. Alternatively, my desires led to the delay of many things that He had for me. Through the course of time, God detoured my blessings and allowed rejection for my protection. The rejection was allowing what needed to be expelled to be expelled. What I wouldn't remove from my life, The Holy Spirit forced out because I wasoperating in disobedience.

THE LEAST LIKELY : LEAH SEASON

2020 was a season of high and lows. In this particular season, I felt related so much to Leah. Leah's story captures her rejection from wanting to be loved correctly and sacrificing all she could in the name of love. In Genesis, chapter 29, Jacob labored for Rachel but, in return, received Leah first. Jacob felt so deceived, but his previous actions of deception were repeated. They allowed him to be on the other end of deception. Leah conceived several children from Jacob. She thought that the more she conceived, the more she surpassed her sister; it would allow Jacob to love her even more. It wasn't so. Jacob still loved Rachel and continuously proved his love for her. Jacob worked so hard for Rachel that seven years seemed like days. If the years seemed liked days, imagine how a month felt. It was all worth it for him.

But what about Leah? In Genesis 29:17, Leah's description wasn't the best to those who looked at her in the flesh. The Bible said Leah had weak eyes, and Rachel was a sight to see. Can you imagine how Leah may have looked at her sister, wishing she received the same love her sister received?

As women, how many of us desired and wanted someone so badly only to be rejected? After countless times of being left, we continue to pour our love into someone, hoping they would change one day. Leah did everything possible to catch the eye of her husband; She even bribed her sister to have a night with Jacob in exchange for the mandrakes Reuben had found for his mother, Leah. For those of you who are unfamiliar with mandrakes. Mandrakes increase fertility. It aided in conception, especially at that time.

Leah´s lineage is the lineage of Christ. Her rejection was part of the process to conceive destiny that would happen after her. My heart aches for Leah. What she endured was my fate these past few years. In 2017, the Holy Spirit laid on my heart a gentleman that had been a childhood friend since high school. I had always been in awe and in love with him. We have 20 years of history, on and off. We always stayed connected throughout the years like there was never any disconnect during our course of time. Somehow, we lost touch within the past few years. The last time we were in one another's presence was in 2014. Coincidently, our children attended the same schools, and we crossed paths at an event. Shortly afterward, we lost touch, and the Holy Spirit placed him in my thoughts again. The thoughts had become so intense that I would sleep, and the Holy Spirit would arrest me in the wee hours of the morning. A mutual connection informed me of his incarceration. I made several attempts to try and locate him and was unable to pinpoint his whereabouts. I had been searching for him through the local and state prison sites. At the time, I had recently left a bad relationship. I was cheated on and rejected by someone else. My heart wasn't into searching for KF on how I should be searching him in the prison systems. I was so focused on healing myself. My healing was a priority.

On May 16th, 2017, The Holy Spirit had arrested me. I was unable to sleep and was given clear insstructions from The Holy Spirit to search for KF. I searched the Federal Bureau of Prisons website and was able to locate him. I wrote a heartfelt letter at 5:55 am explaining my search and reminding him of who he was in the Kingdom. Later on that day, I went to the post office to send off the letter. I remember that day ever so clearly. I was in line at the post office. The line had extended outside the entrance. I prepared to be there for a while. I recollect being in line; while I was waiting, a postal worker asked, "Is there anyone who needs stamps?" I replied, "I do." He signaled me to the front of the line. I had been last in line and was now first. I asked, "How much?" He replied, "It's free." God had shown me the favor that rested upon me and reminded me that the rest of my days would be like this. I remember leaving the post office filled with an indescribable joy. The type of pleasure was equivalent to Elizabeth's womb leaping in the presence of Mary. That was the joy I felt that day.

Three days went by, and I received a call from him. My letter met him with warmth, and I was ecstatic. I was delighted to know he was well and in good spirits despite his situation. We remained in constant communication through calls and emails. One of our first email correspondences led me to believe he felt the same way I did. Affectionately known as KF, he spent four years incarcerated. I reconnected with him in his last year and a half. We'd email one another and communicate via the telephone. To be honest, I was ridin' for him. I was sending him money for his books and more.

I also got his documents to allow him to have proper documentation to complete his appeals. No one could measure the amount of heart and effort I was putting into it. I was going hard. I was going "Leah" hard. Despite all that was going on in my life, I still managed to make things happen expeditiously. Granted, I assumed I had a place in his heart and a title, with all that was going on. He reached out to his family and informed them of who I was and how I had been a blessing in his life. I had to have meant something. A man's mother wouldn't reach out to you and ask to see you, right? I was in communication with his brother also. They were curious about who I was in his life. In my mind, if I were relevant, I would never have to state who I was.

Around this time, I was transitioning. I was looking for a new place to reside. I was currently living in the hood. I was living in Dania, and an unknown assailant had broken into my home several times. I had this conversation with KF. He was excited that I was looking into another area to relocate. He implied that he was excited about finding a new home for us. At the moment, I thought he might be serious about us. I had my share of doubts; it is normal. The connection I felt was unique. We spent most of our days doing Bible devotionals and fasting together. I would share my dreams, and he would share his. He would make mention that I was part of his plans, and he promised that he would spend more time with me when he returned home. Everything that tried to break me, I expressed openly to him, and there wasn't any judgment. He always reminded me that whatever transpired in my life was for a purpose.

I prayed to God for so many years about the ideal man I'd married, and what he would provide matched who KF was. The attributes I wanted in a man were: street smarts, book smarts, and a Man of God. Incredibly, one who knew the Word of God. The more we communicated, the more I saw a reflection of my prayers answered. Very often, KF and I would have Biblical conversations. Many of our discussions would encircle King Solomon and Queen Sheba. We went deep into the scriptures. He referred to us as the modern-day King Solomon and Queen Sheba. Regardless of the words he spoke, doubt still existed.

I began to have dreams of other women he was entertaining. Previously, he exposed a discourse between him and his counselor. He stated, his counselor referred to him as a womanizer. When I heard those words come out of his mouth, it was an instant red flag. He explained that he had multiple women listed as contacts, but he quickly responded that there was no close connection with them. I was feeling swindled in the back of my mind, and I knew that the dreams God was showing me were a revelation of what was currently happening. There were friends of mine connected to him on social media. A few of them saw some disturbing things implying that he was in a current relationship. I had a handful of friends that were his followers on social media. They were trying to protect my peace after all that I had endured in my past... from domestic violence to sexual abuse. If I didn't know how Leah felt in Genesis 29 and 30, I was starting to feel the beginning stages of it.

I would continue to ask God to confirm if KF was for me, and I would always receive answers. The answers were positive, but in the natural, they didn't reflect the promise. I was heavily into the church, seeking God's will and purpose. I had now become celibate and decided that I would save myself for my helpmate. Time was drawing near to KF's release from prison. I had moved into a safer neighborhood with my children. Everything was progressing as it should, but I noticed a change. I wasn't receiving as many calls and emails from KF. I didn't understand how we went from communicating almost every hour to now days went by without us speaking.

By then, problems started surfacing in my life. I had a lot on my plate. When things began to take a turn for the worst in my life, BOP released KF from federal prison in September of 2018. The Holy Spirit revealed he would be released in September. Instantly I checked the records, and needless to say, he was released. He was already placed in a halfway house. There were so many emotions running throughout my mind. I was sad, happy, but most of all, upset that I didn't receive a call from him immediately. A month had gone by, and he had been very standoffish. There was always an excuse as to why I couldn't see him. The more I asked questions, the more he continued to build a wall. Immediately after his release, I went on an intense fast because I knew what God was preparing me for; I would need to be mentally vigorous and capable of handling it. I received a call from KF and what I dreaded to hear is what I heard. His explanation for his distance was that he had to explain to his child's mother that they weren't together, and she thought they were together. Then, he told me he knew he could tell me this without me breaking down because I was spiritually fit! Who says that? The whole time I had been competing with Rachel. There would be many more Rachels to come.

After receiving the devastating news, someone who is no longer connected with me decided to meddle on his page and watch his moves. Their hidden motive was to find joy in seeing me hurt. They forwarded photos of KF's page with a woman who had access to his Instagram page.

She referred to herself as "His Wife.' Multiple images of her were on his page. I sank into a deep depression. I had begun to drink every day. The home that I was making and preparing for his arrival was for nothing. How did I get played, again? How did I not see the signs? I saw the signs but avoided them because I thought I was wrong. There has been a time in our lives that we have overlooked signs because of feelings. In hindsight, I was regretting manythings.

In my mind, I was saying, "If I do a little more, he will love me more." I no longer was celibate. I was taking KF to and from work, which was a 2-hour commute daily. The disrespect continued as I exhausted myself to prove my worthiness. I was witnessing interactions with him on social media with other women I was connected to. He was admiring their bodies and making advances publicly. In addition to the advances, he was asking them out on dates. I cried daily, witnessing these hurtful acts. I felt humiliated. I never had to search, and God always revealed his motives and activity. I was the one who was there. I didn't comprehend why rejection seemedto be chasing me.

I can visualize Leah's pain. I know she looked at her body and compared it to other women. During this period, I gained excessive weight; I was 250 pounds. Although I didn't resemble the weight, I had become very insecure with the women he found interest in. I was comparing my body to theirs and finding everything wrong with me. I had become self-conscious about my weight. I obtained a membership at a gym to receive group training. I was losing weight, but his eyes were on all the Rachels. No matter how hard I prayed for him and with him, it still didn't bring him closer to my heart. My temple was the mandrake that I used to bribe him. I felt as if I didn't have anything else to show or offer. I was giving more and more of my body to him. The more I gave myself, the stronger the soul tie became. As time went by, he became more blatantly upfront with what he was doing. Suddenly, he would reveal that he was dating someone and how his child's mother would be upset and how she crossed paths with the other woman. As he would mention these things, The Holy Spirit would calmly told me not to react in front of him.

Instead, I would cry, pray, and pick up a bottle. KF lacked emotion; he wasn't an empath and had no discernment of what he was doing to my spirit. I am an empath, so it is very different when it comes to my emotions. I started to have dreams about his child's mother violently approaching me.

Within less than 24 hours of the vision, the very same things The Holy Spirit revealed happened. In particular, I was sitting in the car with KF, and he immediately jumped out of my vehicle after watching her surveying his house. She made a U-turn at the stop sign and tried to run into my car. I turned down the volume on the radio. She proudly boasted that she was with him the night before and screamed expletives. As she was arguing with him, I heard the pain in her voice as she called him a user. I didn't agree with any of her actions, but I felt her pain. I knew what she was feeling. Again, I was competing with another Rachel. The drive that night was awkward. A million thoughts were racing through my mind. I was replaying the conversations we shared. I was trying to add up the inconsistencies.

Several comparisons of situations I endured were similar to what I witness that evening. Truthfully, this wasn't the first altercation with a woman. I reflect on my experiences and discussions. I couldn't help but think, *maybe he is a womanizer*. What did I get myself involved with? My heart was in too deep. KF was the master at the gift of gab, and I was always great at recognizing it with other people.

Nonetheless, I became naive to his tactics. Loyalty has been the pinnacle of any relationship I formed with anyone, whether friendship or romantic relationship. My observation with KF revealed that his commitment was with those who hadn't been loyal to him. Those who were worthy of his loyalty, he reciprocated with heartache.

Leah was so unloved and rejected! In Genesis 29:30, it says, "Jacob had intercourse with Rachel also, and he loved her more than Leah." The pain in that one verse taps you into the pain of Leah. Leah always felt second best to Rachel. That is precisely how I felt! I was second best to the women who publicly flaunted their bodies as assets, second best to the strip clubs, and second best to anything that kept his focus on God. I prayed and fasted so many times. I grew weary, but I still prayed. I knew God was working.

Amid the pandemic in 2020, I had a fresh start. I relocated into a new area in March. God was shifting things. The name of the property was the same as the River Jordan in Hebrew, "Yarden." Yarden means, "descender, flow down, fertility, and garden of God." Not to mention, my apartment number symbolizes new beginnings. The same month of my relocation, I conceived a child with KF. After 20 years, I conceived. It was more than a fling to me; I had feelings that laid dormant inside me for decades.

Secretly, I wanted his child, and I finally felt like God had shown me grace. Reminiscing when I told him, I was elated that I was carrying a little person who had his DNA. I shared the news with him, and he was stunned after 20 years it happened. It still plays in my mind how he placed his hand on my stomach and kissed it. I was embracing that I was going to be a mother again and ecstatic. Shortly after the news, I suffered a miscarriage on Easter weekend. I was devastated and emotionally distraught. I was already mentally prepared for a baby. The due date was saved on all my calendars. I even had subscriptions to track my pregnancy.

I couldn't believe I was losing our baby. I'd had several miscarriages, but this one sucked the life out of me! Amid the pandemic, this was happening. I'll never forget being in that cold hospital where the doctors were running tests and checking my HCG levels. They returned to the room to tell me my levels had dropped. I was told to prepare to lose my child. The very same child that I was rejoicing over. I couldn't understand why this was happening again. As a result of the pandemic, you weren't allowed to have anyone in the room, which was understandable. After receiving the news, I slowly put on my clothes and dried my tears. I walked to my car and cried. Everything was moving in slow motion. I remember texting KF telling him the news. His response, "Damn." The drive that evening seems like it took forever. As soon as I returned home, I wept in my bed.

I cried myself to sleep and saturated my pillow with tears. That was the beginning of my nervous breakdown and depression. I dealt with the whole situation alone. I called KF to vent and to cry, but he never responded. I grieved our baby alone, and the more I was alone, the deeper I sank into depression. The process was so painful physically, emotionally, and spiritually. I suffered in silence, and I watched KF publicly live his life through social media. He continuously gave attention to those who didn't even acknowledge or care for him. There I was dealing with pain and needing someone to talk to. I needed him. I was carrying his child, and he treated me like a random groupie. I thought of all the times I covered him in prayer and all the times I came through for him, only to be treated like a nobody. I deserved more - way more than what was handed to me.

I didn't hear from KF for two, nearly three months. Since that incident, I've never been the same, and I've never looked at him the same. The person I was looking at and dealing with was emotionally traumatized. KF was emotionally detached. He was incapable of expressing his feelings. I discerned that he grew up in a household where he was told men weren't supposed to cry. Somewhere in his childhood, what he did to me was done to him. He returned the damage that was done to him, and in the process, it damaged me. But the blessing about the hurt was it created this book, and it produced the title of this book. This was my Leah season, and this was the rebirth of me. It took something so devastating for me to write my first book. Although I'm not fully healed from the situation, writing about it is my therapy.

I would have never thought that someone I knew for over 20 years would do this to me. But just like Ecclesiastes 1:9 says, "There is nothing new under the sun." The rejection was in the lineages of Jesus. Leah experienced it, and it was passed on. As I read Leah's story in this current season, she has become one of my new favorites. I relate to her so deeply because I know what it's like to give your heart and want someone to love you, but they just don't comprehend how to love you the same way because they never experienced true love. Their idea of love was misconstrued, and they're not even emotionally capable of expressing their love for people. I thought I could change it, but I finally let go and gave it to God. The more I tried, the more I hurt myself. The more I intervened, the more I delayed God's healing in his life. Leah had a purpose, and even though she felt unloved, she conceived purpose into this world that allowed many people to be saved even when she felt unworthy.

Lost It All To Gain: The Job Experience

Job, a man of God from the land of Uz had unstoppable faith. He went through seasons of suffering. Job went through several losses without having a chance to process and grieve naturally. He lost his oxen, his servants, his camels, and his children. During his loss, he went to the ground and worshipped. He didn't sin and charge God with wrongdoing. In Job chapter 1, we experience Job's disasters, and we wept with him when he endured in faith. Job was an honorable man who offered burnt sacrifices for his children if they sinned or cursed God in their hearts. Satan seems so confident that Job would turn his back on God and lose faith when he lost everything. That wasn't the case. He was tested with God's permission, but not a finger was supposed to touch his servant Job. I can connect with Job, and I am familiar with what it is like to go through a season of losses, especially when the losses keep happening back-to-back. I understand what it is like wanting to catch your breath after each blow that life has thrown you.

In 2012, I lost everything. My whole life changed from a knock at my door by Haines City Police Department. The Officers who were at my doorstep arrived at my home a little after 7 o'clock PM. I opened the door and one of the officers spoke and said he received a call from my fiancé, who he referred to as my boyfriend. He questioned if him and I had got into a verbal altercation. I explained to Officer Adams that we were fine and that my fiancé was not there. My children and I were alone and they were watching television. I remember the officer being very vexed and I cracked my door open slightly so that he can see my children and I were not in any eminent danger. After explaining to the officers that everything was fine, one of the officers asked me to come outside. I replied that I would not go outside and that I was tending to my children. The then asked to come in. I replied that he was not able to come in. I remember telling him without a warrant or a probable cause that he was not allowed in my home. I further explained to him that there wasn't problem and that he may leave. I proceeded to close the door and the officer forcefully placed his hand on the door and prevented me from closing it. The officer became combative and stated that he did not require a warrant to enter my home and that he will enter my home without one. I explained to officer that he was not able to do so. The other officer stood behind the other officer silently the whole time. I felt intimidated and threatened. At that very moment I felt this situation wouldn't end well. Before I closed the door the officer became very irate. Especially after I explained he didn't have a warrant. I remember both officers forcing their way into my home afterwards. I didn't put up a fight. As far as Im concerned, Im black. It was already against me. I walked into my kitchen to get some bananas for my children that were on top of my microwave. I was prepping dinner for my children who were 3 and 5 at te time. As I was standing in the kitchen I explained to the officer that everything was fine and that he needed to vacate my home. He loudly refused. I was in the kitchen washing my hands for a brief moment. As I was washing my hands one officer stood to my right directly in front of the sink and the other officer stood behind me to the left near the stove by the trash receptacle which was also a small portion of the dining room area. I felt very unsettled. Something felt awkward in my spirit. I turned around and plucked 2 bananas the top of the microwave and made way towards the living room. As I stepped towards the Living Room my phone rang. It was vibrating. I saw that it was my fiancé who had called. I had a really bad feeling and was really scared so I quickly answered the call with one of the officers behind me. I remember having one banana in each hand so that they can visibly see what was in my hand. As I stepped out into the Living Room area, I remember still seeing one officer from the side of my eye behind me. As I made it to the living room and my children stretched their arms waiting for me to give them their bananas. Within seconds I was being grabbed from the shoulders and arms. My wrist were being twisted. I was crying and asking, "What did I do wrong"? I was trying to feed my children. I was slammed into a closet and my body was sliding as I tried to pick myself up. But the closet door had caved in and the officer continued to use excessive force on me. I was pleading with him asking him why over and over. I pleaded with him not to do this in front of my kids. I stared at my children crying and my children crying as they stared at me. I was crying and screaming that they were hurting me. I screamed to the officer that he was mishandling me incorrectly and that he was man handling me. I explained to him there was no reason for this and pleaded with him not to do this in front of my children. Handcuffs were placed. My fiancé was on the phone listening to the whole attack. During this whole ordeal I watched the other officer standing with his hands in his pocket. He did nothing. He didn't intervene. He was very non chalant. I remember being dragged outside by the officer. I plead and cried with the officer that I didn't know anyone out here because I recently relocated and my children would have no one to care for them. I cried that this wasn't right. I questioned the officers if my arrest was because I am feeding my children. After crying the residents of the apartment complex and the surrounding areas were coming out to witness was taking place. No one came to my defense. I kept crying telling him there is a possibility that I might be pregnant. As the officer dragged me to the patrol car my sandal had fallen off and detached from the bottom. I looked at him and begged him not do this. He asked me to enter the unit. I cried and said please let me just stay with my children until my fiancé gets here. The officer pulled out his taser and then said if I didn't enter the vehicle that he would tase me. I entered the vehicle quickly in fear my children would witness this senseless act. I didn't make any physical move to suggest that I was a threat to him. Not one time when the handcuffs were placed on me. Not to mention either of the officers read me my Miranda Rights. After I was placed in the vehicle the officer walked back into my apartment. He returned to ask me my name. I did not respond. I wasin a state of shock.

Both officers did an unauthorized search in my apartment. The officers returned to the unit and stated they were charging me with a Felony battery on a LEO. I explained to Officer Adams with this charge I will lose my Job and never be able to work with the special needs population again. He proceeded to asked had I ever been arrested and how long ago was it? I replied it had been 12 years. He said with that the judge will throw it out and I will be out by tomorrow. I was still in disbelief that I was being arrested when I was te victim of a battery. The officer got a hold of my ex fiancé and told me that he would arrive in an hour to be with my kids. Sometime had passed and the officers approached me about documents in my home. He also explained if I let him know the reason that I wouldn't have to go to jail. I looked towards the front of the patrol vehicle and did not reply. So he closed the vehicle and went back into the apartment. The other officer came out and asked me some questions, I did not reply. He left and went back in the apartment. While I was sitting in the patrol vehicle I observed both officers laughing and joking with some men that lived in the apartment complex as they left my children unattended inside my home. They were given bottled water and also tasted some red liquid off the cap of the bottle with their fingers given by a resident of the complex. I was sitting in the vehicle for a while. I was extremely hot; the vehicle wasn't running and all the windows were up. By then I knew I had been in the vehicle for more than an hour. I couldn't believe what was happening to me.

The officer was using his radio at the rear of the car. He entered the patrol vehicle and was copying and pasting a format for a police arrest report. He typed in my name and listed the charges as Battery and Assault on a LEO and Resisting Arrest with Violence. I witnessed him typing the charges into laptop, I asked him in what way did I assault him if my back had been facing him. Why was excessive force used for having 2 bananas in my hand to feed to my children? He said that I touched him. Which was absurd. A black woman weight 175 with 2 male officers present, the report was preposterous. After he was finished typing his report he notified his partner. Afterwards they notified DCF to remove my children from the home because my ex fiancé didn't arrive at the time expected. Before he left I begged to see my children. My son latched on to my shoulders not wanting to let go. My daughter gave me a kiss. He walked them back to the apartment to leave the other officer to watch them until DCF arrived. The officer entered the vehicle and drove off. I remember I asked the officer, "Why are you leaving?" He wasn't suppose to leave until my ex fiancé arrived." As he drove off I told him that what he had done was wrong. I told him my children don't have any close relatives or know anyone out here. Again I told him with these charges I will never be able to work with special needs or children for the rest of my life. He never responded. We arrived at The Haines City Police Department. I was kept in the holding cell. When I arrived I asked that my ex fiancé be called and the officer said it went directly to the voicemail. The officer responded to the voicemail as if my ex fiancé actually answered when he realized it was an answering service he replied, "I hate this stupid voicemail'". A female officer then came to the cell and searched me. My pockets were checked. My ring was removed, but my earrings remained in my ears. I estimate that I was held at the police station for about an hour. The removed me from the holding cell. Before he placed me in the patrol vehicle he apologized for all that had happened. He placed me in the patrol vehicle. As he pulled out the parking lot, he made a stop. His Sergeant was in the parking lot before the exit of the police station. The officer rolled down the front right passenger window. The Sergeant approached the front right passenger side of the vehicle and said my ex fiancé had notified them. Also that my exvfiancé was about 30 minutes away. He explained to the officer that my ex fiancé worked in loss prevention and he would be there shortly. They mentioned if he arrived before DCF he is able to that he would be able to watch my children without DCF interfering. They also stated if he arrived after them hopefully they will arrange it where he can have custody of the kids until I am released. I told the Sergeant that officer didn't read me my Miranda rights. The sergeant replied he doesn't have to because he didn't ask you any questions, which I thought was really awkward because he did question me. The officer drove off. We later arrived at the Central Booking Station in a nearby city. The officer told the staff and the nurse about me possibly being pregnant. I was asked to go in the cell. I was asked questions pertaining to medical history. I was still under shock of the misconduct I received. I didn't respond to any questions. I was traumatized. I was asked to place my hands on the wall and my knees on the seating area with my back facing them. I was searched asked to remove my clothes. The result of not answering questions about my medical history caused me to be on suicide watch. The nurse on duty explained that it would be worse for me because I might be placed in a mental institution and that I would be here longer than expected. I told them I want to be with my kids and we don't know anyone here. I replied, "This is not fair." I was issued my Jail uniform with panties. I was placed in another cell awaiting transport. Later on, approximately after midnight we were transported in the County Jail vehicle. We arrived at the final transport destination close to 1 am or about 1 am. We were walking through the jail and we made it to the final building. I was told that the three women I was handcuffed with, including myself would all get a final appearance in the morning or after lunch. One of the officers stated that I was on suicide watch. I was stunned. I questioned, "Why?" They stated, "They didn't know. I was brought into isolation and was asked to removeall my clothing. My earrings still remained in my ear; my lace front wig with my stocking cap still remained. These items were a potential harm but they failed to remove it or recognize it as a threat. I was given a blanket to place on the concrete floor and anti suicide mock. But the Velcro on the mock wasn't any good. So I remained naked. I sat down and cried myself to sleep wondering about my children. I waited anxiously for my first appearance so that I can prove my case. I was awakened by a male officer who approached the door of the cell. I was in asking, "Why didn't he have any paper work on me." Breakfast and lunch had passed and I saw one of the female officers and asked, "When would they be gathering individuals for first appearance?" I explained to her that an officer told me that I would be on that list. She gave me an attitude and stormed off. I remember crying and asking for someone to help me and give me answers so I can be home with my children. Finally another officer that was really kind told me to calm down. She said a psych counselor would come and evaluate me and then I could be removed from suicide watch and that I would be able to make a call. While I waited to make a call, I showered. The same officer that gave me the information informed me later that day my bond had been posted. I was so excited and cried. So I waited by the door until the officer returned. Finally she returned to give me clothes and undergarments to get dressed. I quickly got dressed and walked in handcuffs with another inmate. We were all transferred back to central booking. It was 3 women inmates including myself and one male inmate. We arrived and were given a brown paper bag that contained all of our belongings. The other female inmates I was with were given their clothes. They had me on hold because they had never taken my fingerprints or my mug shot upon arrival. Once they had my mug shot in the system, I was able to change. When the other inmates and I were finished changing, we were asked to go to the booth for our court and bond information. While I was waiting a male officer motioned with his hands for me to come to the area where the fingerprints were conducted. He input my fingerprints in the system and I went back in line to wait for my information. I was given my ex fiancé's number and told to call him as soon as possible. She said he was very concerned and that he had been calling constantly.The same man who was concerned was the one who caused all of this!

Shortly after I was given documents of when my court date would be held. I signed documents pertaining to my court date and bond. Before my release I asked the clerk to use the phone. I placed a phone call to inform my exvfiancé I will be out shortly about 630 pm. After my phone call I was placed back in the holding cell, I was waiting for the final call to do a final fingerprint of the index and middle finger followed by our signature. The other inmates were given back the rest of their property and we were escorted out the doors of the facility. The time was close to 7pm. I was finally being reunited with my children. The scariest part about this situation was back in the presence of ex fiancé who was a narcissist, manipulator and abuser. He was the whole mastermind behind this. He had to mae sure my children were ok. His reputation was on the line. You would think after this situation t got better it didn't. I was fired from my job at Orange County public schools. I moved back home to Miami. That season was burdensome for me and for the next 2 year I would be fighting this case. I was asked to take pleas and probations. I didn't. was obedient to God´s voice and was found not guilty.

In 2014, I was starting fresh. I beat a ten-year prison sentence where I was falsely accused of battery on law enforcement when in actuality, I no longer had to drive from South Florida to Central Florida. During those periods, I was arrested for open warrants for failing to miss court, and so much more. The trauma that I endured from that situation was heartbreaking. 2014 was also the year my divorce was finalized from the man that tried to kill me. Unfortunately, after all the abuse I endured I married him when I moved back home. In return he turned witness for prosecution in my case and missed every hearing. Aint God good!

Although 2014 was just as chaotic as 2012, things seem to be turning around. A new career was on the rise. I was attending school to be a make-up artist. At that moment, I was living with a relative who was helping me get on my feet. It wasn't easy. The things I endured during that time of reestablishing myself were painful. I was dealing with cyberbullying from my ex-husband and dealing with the deception of a relative who was secretly telling him things that were private in my life. I was trying to heal, but it was so hard to recover when the person that caused you pain made it their purpose to make you miserable for leaving. Not to mention dealing with the scrutiny from former classmates about the abuse. Emotionally, I was suffering from depression. In the midst of it all, I knew God had a purpose behind every scenario. Despite all that was going on, I was still shouting and singing that God was good. My faith never wavered, and every test made my faith grow more robust and showed me exactly who God was in my life.

2013 was insane; my ex-husband was always calling DCF and having them visit my cousin's home in an effort to have my kids taken away. By the grace of God, favor was over my life and my children. DCF was able to recognize that this was somebody who was being vicious. In addition to all that was going on, my relative grew in fear of me living with them. I became a victim of a real-life stalker. My life was shifting again. Imagine being a nomad moving from place to place. This time I was in a domestic violence shelter in fear for my life and with nowhere else to go. I completed my make-up artistry school from a homeless shelter. It was strenuous, but I did it. I finished the first assignment. All the obstacles that I went through in the process genuinely showed God's hand was over my life. The scripture that comes to mind for that time is Job 13:15, "though he slay me, yet will I hope in him; I will surely defend my ways to his face." This is how deep my faith was and the enemy wanted to test it, just like he tested Job.

I was being tested again; I found myself in a situation where another child assaulted my daughter at the shelter. I confronted a parent about the situation, which led to a verbal altercation and damaged property. Immediately after the quarrel, my family and I were removed from the shelter. Once again, we were homeless. We were escorted out of the facility by law enforcement. All of our belongings were squeezed into a small compact vehicle. My children and I were forced out the faciliy. I remember vacating the premises and parking under the shade. In my mind, I was to figure out where we would go. At the moment, it seemed impossible. I'd run out of options. There was one person that came into mind that I had recently reconnected with from my past. I immediately reached out to her, and she opened her doors for my kids and I to lay our heads. There we were, laying on the sofa, a sectional all three of us. One of the most challenging moments of our lives was that the babies were so little but so humble through it all. The situation was so uncomfortable for my children and me, but we made the best of it. That situation didn't last forever.

Later on, the person who allowed us to stay in her home tried to do witchcraft on me, and another altercation occurred because of pure jealousy. My children and I, once again, were displaced. I remember crying profusely, just waiting on an answer from God.

During the short time at that home, I got acquainted with another family who opened their doors to my children and me. We stayed there until a waiting list opened up at a family shelter. We finally got the call before Thanksgiving. In early October, we were put into a family shelter. Everything we owned was in my car. All we had was clothes. Many people questioned why I was going through what I was going through repeatedly? Many asked, "Why does she still believe in God and she's suffering?" People wanted me to denounce God, and that was one thing I would not do. Regrettably, people around me were not able to endure the mystery of my suffering. Just like Job's friends blamed his suffering on him, this was what I was going through in this season.

People often believe when calamity happens in your life, it is deserved, but they don't realize it's a test. In the New Testament, in the book of James, chapter 1, verses 2-4, it says, "Consider it pure joy my brothers and sisters when you face trials of many kinds because you know that the testing of your faith produces perseverance. Let perseverance finish its work so that you may be mature and complete, and not lacking anything." What many people don't realize is what I was going through was simply a test. In situations of hurt and pain, trials and tribulations, we often succumb to other people's bits of advice. What has God put on you that you felt like it was your fault or other people blamed you? Things we go through are all testing of our faith. We have to observe it in a way that we were strong enough to receive the trials because God knew we would be able to handle the temptation from the enemy.

I had to go through many storms and pass certain tests to get to where I had to go. For that reason, God granted me favor at the shelter. Almost immediately after being placed in the shelter, my life shifted. I was moving in faith. I was interviewing with Mac cosmetics for the fourth time. Within a month, I was now being placed into a brand-new apartment that fit my income. The only thing I was waiting on was the second form of employment to help me be stable enough to pay my bills. God made it happen on Thanksgiving Day in 2014, exactly a month after being in the shelter. God blessed me with a two-bedroom apartment. The same day I got the apartment's approval was the same day MAC Cosmetics called me and told me I had a job. I had gone through several interviews with them throughout the years, and in the final interview, I was given the position. I remembered my prayer to God, and I simply stated to him, if this is not where you need me to be, God, close the doors and opportunities. God immediately opened doors to show me that I was in the right place. As soon as I received confirmation about my new employment with MAC, instantly I packed my things. I was so ecstatic to be finally having a place of my own with my children

Can you imagine what it's like to share a space with 15 families? Everything you do is under the public eye. Family meals are not intimate. Everything is done in public. We were finally getting the fresh start we deserved. It was finally happening. We didn't even have to sleep on anyone's floor or living room. Finally, our lives were coming together. I finally had a job and a roof over my head.

There was one dilemma: having childcare for my children while I was going to work. My children were five and six at the time. There were days I had to leave them home alone because childcare hadn't kicked in yet. There were days that I had to bring them with me and let them fall asleep in the car while I worked. Leaving them home wasn't an option; the neighborhood I lived in wasn't safe, and my home and other homes were broken into repeatedly. I remember being excited to get the job, but dreading to go because my I had no one to care for my kids. I didn't have options on who to leave my children with and I didn't trust certain people because I would hear how they talked about watching other people's children related to them. So, I could only imagine what would be said about mine.

One day while going to work, my life changed forever. It was New Year's Eve 2014. I exited into the parking garage and was greeted immediately by the local police department. In the back of a police car were my two children screaming and crying. I was placed under arrest, and my kids were getting ready to be placed in the custody of The Department of Children and Family Services. I couldn't believe what was happening before my eyes. It was just a matter of days until childcare would kick in, and now I had lost my children. The thought of us being homeless again was bothering me to the core. I refused to let it happen again, but somehow, Iwas dealing with another loss.

The enemy knew my kids were are my source of strength; now they were gone. What was I going to do? I remember waving bye to my children from the patrol car, not knowing when I would see them again. My heart was torn, and I was lost without my children. That evening, I was placed in a holding cell before transferring to the main facility, and I remember the correction officers' cruel words. I remember them telling me how much of a bad mother I was. Visualize your heart already being pulled out from your soul because your children were taken from you. You're dealing with the words of people who didn't understand your situation and what you went through. It was equivalent to the abuse I endured from my ex-husband. That's how the pain felt. In a way, I was prepared for this situation, God had shown me in a dream that this would happen, but I didn't believe it then.

My children were now placed with my younger sister that I wasn't on good terms with due to the inappropriate interactions with my ex-husband. I was in no place or in a position to say where my kids would be placed temporarily. They were in the only place that wouldn't allow them not to be separated. For the next few months, I would have supervised visitation with my kids. I had to prove I had the income to be able to take care of them. Child Net conducted an investigation of my home to make sure I was complying with the rules and regulations.

I returned to work through all the adversity and the humiliation. My co-workers circulated my mug shots around and publicly humiliated me. I remained resilient. Eventually, that make-up counter removed me from the schedule, and I went to another make-up counter to get hours. As long I was able to provide proof of employment, the kids would return home. A portion of the agreement with the courts was also for me to attend parenting classes. I was doing just about anything for my babies to come home. The trials started surfacing again. I had a new car that was damaged, and now I was on the verge of losing my place. If I couldn't keep my place, my children wouldn't be able to return home. I found myself looking for local resources with grant assistance programs to help me keep my place. There was so much difficulty and sabotage behind it, but God made a way.

The already broken relationship with my estranged sibling who had my children was completely severed after an altercation. They immediately requested the removal of my kids from their home. Aside from that, the grant assistance clerks tried to sabotage my assistance application. I dealt with so much pain in silence, and I still kept my faith in God. Loss after loss, and I still kept my head high.

At the end of 2015, almost a year to the date I lost the children, they were returned home. I relived the torment that I endured every day, and I still relive it. The babies were back home, and I was just getting back into the flow of things. I received financial assistance from a few sources. God made a way out of no way. Although I didn't have a vehicle, I was delighted to have my children home. It gave me a greater appreciation for the smaller things in life. During those seasons of loss, I was promoted to another make-up counter and given more hours. Those times were suitable for me because the kids weren't home, but I knew when the kids returned, the schedule would have to change. Subsequently, my dream job ended up becoming my worst nightmare, and in 2016 I was forced to step down from a permanent position. I decided to become a freelance make-up artist, which would allow me to pick and choose my schedule for my children's sake. Although it would be difficult to solidify hours, I had peace of mind knowing that my kids would be able to see me. The schedule allowed me to become a sports mom. My daughter was cheerleading, and my son played football. It gave me such joy to witness these moments and not be overworked and miss the many important occasions.

Also, in 2016, I started my non-profit organization, Virtuous Hearts Inc. The pain that I endured from my sufferings allowed purpose to be birthed. I knew I wanted to help people in the less fortunate communities and provide resources for domestic violence victims. God was taking what I went through to use me to be a vessel for other people. In my downtime, God downloaded in me, and I believed what Philippians 4:13 said, "I Can Do All Things Through Christ Who Strengthens Me."

I spent the majority of 2016 without a car, but rejoicing because of God's goodness. My taxes were audited in that season also, but God had a reason! God saw my heart and how my heart was opened to help people in need, and God allowed me to be still because he knew people would take advantage of me. God wanted me to observe the surroundings of those who were near me in my season loss. He wanted me to take notes and recognize those who genuinely had the character of Christ. The rejection was expelling those who needed to be removed. I was involved in another relationship where I was deeply attached to the family, and everything collapsed. I was rejected by someone who had more, all because I had lost. God was showing me, in my losing season, that He was the closest thing to me. God was the only real friend that stuck by my side through it all. God was rebuilding my strength and set my soul on fire. I was learning the real meaning of peace.

I must confess, it wasn't easy. I cried when God peeled certain people away from life. We have to understand when things don't align with his purpose or his will, he has to dissect them out your life to make room for his glory to be revealed. We don't choose our purpose. Our purpose selects us through the testimony of our lives. God knew what it would be before we were even created. Jeremiah 1:5 - "Before, I formed you in the womb; I knew you, before you were born, I set you apart; I appointed you as a prophet to the nations."

In 2018 things were shifting around for the greater. I was in the process of moving to a better area. I was moving out of the ghetto. The move was significant because my son was enduring a lot of bullying at the current school he was at. We had already transitioned to new schools; all we needed to do was find a place conveniently located near the school. In February 2018, we moved into this nice apartment in a good location. We were finally getting our fresh start. We moved in faith. The place we moved into was quite difficult to get into. Where we were residing at the time did a background check, and I didn't qualify to live there due to my criminal history. My mother did me a huge favor and signed the lease in her name. She helped us get settled in and helped us move; it was a blessing in disguise.

Although we made a huge move on the inside. It didn't feel like home. There was a huge feeling of discomfort inside of me. Before the move, I calculated the finances, and I was able to sustain the apartment. Eventually, it became a struggle to pay rent; I was over-drafting my account and having to replace it. While the financial struggle was taking place, my car was on its last leg, and I had no choice but to purchase a new vehicle. By the grace of God, I was able to get a new vehicle from Carmax with no money down and trade in a vehicle that was no longer working. If that isn't God, I don't know what else to tell you!

After I received the vehicle, we were evicted from our apartment within less than a month. We returned home one day, and the key we always used to unlock the door no longer worked. That was God's way of telling me that chapter was closed, and he was getting ready to place my family and me elsewhere. I remember the feelings and emotions that day. I remember my children crying. I remember my daughter hopping through the window to see if we could retrieve any of our items. I remember her crying and screaming, and she unlocked the door. Everything we owned was gone from our clothes to the furniture… everything. We had nothing; the only thing we had left was the clothes on our backs and the new vehicle in the parking lot. Even the make-up I used to make a living was gone. The dumpster had the remnants of my make-up, but they were no longer of good use.

The first person I was able to call that night when everything went down was KF. I remember I cried my heart out. He was one of the few people that were there. He donated clothes and school supplies to my children, which I was forever grateful for. That evening we had enough money to live in a hotel for at least a month. I was prepared for everything that was happening; God had already shown me what was getting ready to occur. For a moment, I cried, and afterward, I sucked it up and said God is going to replace everything that I've lost, He always had, and he always will.

As we transitioned from an apartment to a hotel, I tried to make the situation as comfortable as possible for the babies. The children's school had to be notified, and they were placed in a program that would donate clothing and shoes to them. I was grateful, if that was my biggest concern. All our belongings were in the trunk. We sorted through our belongings every morning in the car. The hotel no longer was an option. Unfortunately, we had to live with people that we knew temporarily. The children and I shared one room. During that transition, it was difficult. The commute to school and from home was at least an hour and a half daily. Not to mention, the drive to Miami at an additional hour to that. Then there were days when I had late shifts or jobs and could not make it inside the house, and there were days I had to sleep on the beach or in my car. After some time, our living arrangements had expired, and we had less than one week to find proper living arrangements. My spirit was heavy, and I didn't know where God would lead us or take us, but I knew He would never forsake me.

A friend at the time made arrangements for us to live in someone's home, but the agreement was to take care of an elderly quadriplegic woman. The agreement was to be in the house by 10pm every night to give her meds. There were some days it had become tedious because I had long workdays and long school hours. I knew God had placed me there for a reason. My patience was tested, and my kids were placed in positions where they endured a lot of blame. In exchange for assisting with the older woman, I would not have to pay any rent, but eventually, they reneged on that agreement, and that's when God told me it's time for you to go.

When God gave me that word, I started looking for other places to move. Within a week, a realtor found a place three minutes away from the beach. Anyone that knows me knows that the beach is the place where I find solace. The favor of God was over my life in that situation. The apartment he gave me didn't require a background check, and it didn't require any of the extras that I had to go through with the last place that I lost. Not to mention, my apartment was number eight. The number eight Biblically means new beginnings. It signifies resurrection and regeneration. It is the symbol of a new order. Since God placed me in this new apartment, I haven't had any struggles or any financial issues God has provided. In the midst of my moving into this place, a pandemic occurred, and it financially crippled many people, but God allowed me to stay afloat, and He blessed me with a brand-new car, a Mercedes-Benz. He gave me double for my trouble. He placed me in an area that I always desired to be in. Truthfully this was the area he was showing me to move into before moving to the other place that I lost. God will allow you to be rejected and redirected for his purpose. This is the scripture that I live by faithfully. It has been a model of my life, and it will be the model of your life too. Jeremiah 29, verse 11 - "I know the plans that I have for you, plans to prosper you and not to harm you plans to give you a hope and a future."

ABUSED TO BE USED :
MY STORY OF DOMESTIC VIOLENCE

Who was Jesus? Jesus was the son of God, and he was crucified for his sins, but before he was crucified, he led a ministry. He was a carpenter, a teacher, a son, and a friend. Jesus was born in Bethlehem to Mary, who was a Virgin. Before Jesus was even born, his life was in jeopardy. Jesus was loved by many and rejected by many. The Messiah's teaching ministry was done in a way that made other people question him. Christ was rejected before he made his grand entrance on earth! Not to mention those who were close with him in ministry. The rejection was a part of the process for the many souls to be saved. Jesus said it best in Mark 6:4, "A prophet is not without honor except in his own town, among his relatives and in his own home." When you walk with Christ, you are called to be rejected. You will be rejected by those who don't understand. I cried, reading about Jesus' different seasons of rejection. It is when I experiencedit; I understood what it meant to bear the cross.

In spring 2017, my relationship with Christ was restored. I had a sense of urgency to be back in the House of the Lord. I knew there had been a calling on my life, and I knew I needed to be in a place of worship. On one particular Sunday, I posted to social media, and I asked, "Is there a church providing service at a certain time?" Two churches were listed in the comments section, and that day, I did two services. The second church that I attended gravitated to my spirit. As time went by, I noticed my strength wasn't gradual; it catapulted. I began to pray more, fast more, and worship more. 2017 was the year I was falling in love with Christ all over again. My desire and passion for seeking God were immense. I made sure to attend church every Sunday. At midnight, before every service, I would fast just to receive the goodness of the Lord. Worship would play in my car day in and day out. My life was changing in a blink of an eye. My heart longed to have a church home for my family, and I knew God would bring that to fruition.

It wasn't the church that changed me, but it was my desire to grow a relationship with Christ that changed me. In the same manner, God had grown my spiritual gifts, and my discernment grew rapidly. Envision being in church, and you're the only one wearing bold, colorful hair, and you feel in your spirit that you're being judged. As time went by, I was feeling unexcepted and unwanted. The feelings that I felt in the very beginning started to subside. There was a feeling of judgment and a lack of support. Very much what Jesus went through in his ministry.

Prior to becoming a member of the ministry, I had my own ministry called Virtuous Heart, Inc. At the time, the ministry was only a year old, but I was consistent in doing the work of the Lord. I would cater and give meals to the less fortunate community and provide blankets to keep them warm throughout the year. In addition to providing meals, I would also provide services for the women who are in domestic violence shelters year-round. Truthfully, there was a lack of support from the church, not all of the church, but the majority of the church. For a moment, I felt like I belonged, but as time went by, I noticed that something didn't feel right. God began to show me secret conversations in the spirit amongst people in the body of the church, judging my appearance and my purple hair. Granted, I was heavily involved in the ministry and my hunger for Christ was apparent. No one wanted to believe the call on my life. I was eager and humble to serve, but quickly overlooked. The way I worshiped was even questioned if it was authentic and genuine. I started to feel out of place, but I continued to attenduntil God gave me clearance to leave.

I was doing everything I needed me to do. The glory of God was all over my life. In a matter of months, I was even able to pray in the spirit. That was something that I sought God for years. I was involved in the various activities of the church, from the children's ministry to Bible study. Bible study became more horrific by the minute. It seems like at almost every other Bible study, I was targeted about my lifestyle. I was questioned about the places where I ate, even down to my nose ring. There was one particular day during a Bible study, the preacher asked, "Who drinks Starbucks?" Two women in the church pointed directly at me as if it was hilarious. That very day I posted on social media that I was at Starbucks ministering to a woman that God allowed me to be in her presence. For days, God allowed me to pray and intercede for her privately. I publicly shared how I was able to pray for her and her breakthrough. It was so preposterous to me how they would look at where I was at and not look at the blessing behind it. I was able to be there and minister to somebody and pray for them to reach their breakthrough. Instead, they felt I was in a demonic place supporting the devil's ministry. I remember, at the very moment when the preacher targeted me about drinking at Starbucks, how that broke me. Then he stated, sarcastically, that it was devils and that if I wanted to continue putting money in the devil's pockets, by all means, go ahead. But I remember Jesus and what he went through. In Mark 2:15, Jesus sat and had dinner with the tax collectors and the sinners. There were many people that follow him. When the teachers of the law, who were the Pharisees, witnessed him eating with the sinners in tax collectors, they questioned him. Jesus' response in Mark 2:17 was a drop the mic moment. Jesus said, "It is not the healthy who need a doctor but the sick. I have not come to call the righteous, but the sinners." Jesus, his whole ministry caters to the ill, from the prostitutes to the tax collectors.

I knew I was cut from a different cloth and I knew where God was getting ready to take me was different from the mindset of those who are religious. It seems like every time I stepped into the house of the Lord, I was hearing about things not being tolerated in the church. One of the matters discussed was women should not be wearing pants if ushering. I openly wore pants or one-piece romper pant sets. Another bible study topic would be nose piercings. I remember another church member and I being singled out. We were told that our piercing was Hindu, and it symbolized reproductivity. But nothing was mentioned about the Bible scriptures that spoke of nose rings in a not so negative way. (Ezekiel 16:12 & Genesis 24:47) Rebekah was adorned with bracelets and a nose ring by Issac's servant. Everything I was doing was questioning, even my career. My career as a make-up artist is very extensive; I do event make up to special effects make-up. My gifting was referred to as demonic, and it was even suggested that I was into witchcraft.

Time went by, and there was a tugging in my spirit to depart from there. I was real-life dealing with the Pharisees. Everything I did was for the Lord, but somehow, my outside appearance was the biggest problem. For a long time, I was in the dark about their true feelings towards me. Don't get me wrong; it wasn't everyone in the church. It was enough to feel extremely uncomfortable. I know two things about feeling uncomfortable: It either means you are supposed to be there, or it is time to go. In my particular case and God dealing with me, I know it was time for me to go. God had given me two warnings prior to that to make an exit, and I wasn't obedient. The delay made the process more painful. The final draw for me was on a Sunday afternoon service. That particular Sunday, I was over children's Bible study. That day they were giving positions in ministry to certain individuals of the church. At that moment, no one had ever approached me and asked me where I saw myself in the church. But many other people in the church had been approached about where they saw themselves. Already I was starting to feel out of place and rejected because of my appearance. I remember being called from the back of the church, from the room that I was watching over the children. When I arrived in the church, they assigned me to a ministry that wasn't discussed. I remember a form being available upfront as consent to take the position. I was so livid that day. The amount of hurt that I felt was indescribable.

The ministry I was assigned had no affiliation to the church. How did it make me feel? It left me broken. Although it was painful, it took quite some time for me to heal. Did the situation leave emotional scarring? Yes. Did it make me paranoid about the church? Yes, it did. The one thing that I learned was that people with titles are no different than people without. We often put so much on people with titles and portray this image that they can't makeany mistakes.

In that season, God allowed me to see how people operate and how folks with titles are spiritually immature. God was using that very moment to prepare me and show me the kind of people that I would deal with in ministry. I had to be hurt in order to grow. Ironically the very same place that broke me is the very same place that God imparted heavily into me. It wasn't the people that allowed the growth; it was God who honored me in my stillness before it was time for me to leave.

IT WAS ALL APART OF THE PROCESS: REJECTED FOR PURPOSE

Domestic violence can be described as a violent or aggressive behavior that happens within the home, typically involving a violent, abusive spouse or a partner. There are several types of abuse that fall under domestic violence. There is control, physical abuse, sexual abuse, emotional abuse, intimidation, isolation, verbal abuse, and economic abuse. Often people believe that domestic violence can only be physical. That is not necessarily so. People are often educated on how domestic violence falls under different categories. For example, if you're dealing with an individual who is continuously monitoring your calls and devices and making choices on your clothing, that is controlling abuse. Anything involving hitting, kicking, biting, slapping, or shaking is physical. Also, any form of rape, coercion or guilt, or manipulation to force a victim to have sex falls under sexual abuse. Any unwanted sexual experiences fall under that type of abuse. Usually, sexual abuse involves exploitation or making fun of another sexuality or body. In addition to the others, I mention we also have emotional abuse. Emotional abuse involves any insulting or criticizing a victim's confidence. Usually, emotional abuse that ties into the isolation part of the abuse is often closely connected with controlling behaviors. The perpetrator isolates the victim from relationships and from socially being involved with people to prevent them from being exposed. Next, we have verbal abuse, which is threatening name-calling and screaming. The final two forms of abuse are often neglected and not considered as a form of abuse. You have economic abuse and stocking. They are both as volatile as physical and verbal. Economic abuse is controlling financial resources. Financial resources may include spending money on food, rent, and utilities. Stalking is defined as an unwanted pursuit from another person. There are different forms of stalking. You have cyberstalking, which is using technology to stalk, and then you also have a crime that can cause fear without physical injury. Examples of stalking can be the following: kidnapping, criminal mischief, forgery, and criminal impersonation.

All of these forms of abuse were very familiar to me. Almost every relationship that I've been in was abusive. I've experienced being dragged by a car, to almost being thrown out of a car, to a busted lip.

The final draw for me is the relationship with my ex-husband. The year 2009 was a game-changer for me. I became a mother again to my daughter, and I already had a 1-year-old son. This year of my life, I was drawing closer to God. I was attending church regularly, attending mid-services throughout the week, along with Bible study. I was at church so frequently that church members would jokingly laugh about me practically residing in church, that's how much I was there. I was so moved and drawn to getting my relationship back right with God; I was determined and focused.

My life was on track, spiritually. I remember being in such a beautiful peace that nothing could destroy the happiness that I had with God. The peace that resonated with my spirit was unbelievable. I found myself at that time wanting to do nothing but talk about how God had been good to me, and with all the trials that I was enduring, I was still thankful for his goodness and his Mercy. At that time, I was employed with a great government job. I had a great career. I instructed kids with special needs. I was living my life in my mid-twenties. I was living life the way it was intended. I was now enjoying the company of old friends from high

46

school. Having girls' days out and shopping. I was out having dinner on a regular with Friends to clear my mind from the things I was dealing with the father of my kids. I was completely over repairing that relationship. God had already spoken to my heart that it was time to move on, and I listened.

After I moved, things were still a little bit rocky, and around the time, things were rocky. I met my ex-husband at the time. He seems to be the voice of reason when things seem to be going sour. Through my trials and tribulations from 2009 until our 20-year high school reunion, he was there. Although he lived in another county at the time, we managed to keep in contact quite often. During our connection, we lost touch a little bit, but we maintained contact on social media. It was a lot of flirting an exchange of words. In 2010 my house or 20-year reunion took place, and we reconnected from there, we were taking road trips to see each other, and it got more intense.

My feelings were growing intensely for him. Many of the signs were starting to show. The same symptoms that I mentioned of abuse. I had normalized domestic violence in my life, I brushed those signs off. He was already starting to become controlling. There were women in my circle at the time who were very familiar with his abusive traits. He had a history of being violent towards women. They were women who were very familiar with what he had done in the past. When I was heavily involved in church, my mindset was trying to see the best in people and overlook their history. My ex-husband was now trying to control the people that I was speaking with. Most of the time, he explained to me that they were very immature, and they gossiped a lot. Some days, he would come to me and tell me that the women would be talking maliciously about me. When he started those rumors, isolation started to occur not with just the friendships but with family. My eyes were open, my ears were open, but they weren't receiving. I noticed that people were unfriending me in real life and on social media, and the same people he was telling me to stay away from; he was befriending them. A lot of the information he was receiving was frommy younger sister which was vey disheartening.

After nearly a year of being together, I relocated to Central Florida to be with him. Surprisingly, with all the signs that revealed themselves in the process, I still left. I didn't want to believe that what I was seeing was unraveling before my eyes. So many things had taken place before the move. The first indicators were verbal abuse and control. During the course of time, a series of events took place that nearly led to my spiritual demise. Every form of abuse that I mentioned is what I endured in the seasons of that relationship. During the relationship, I found out that my ex-husband was juggling two relationships. He was residing with the mother of his child and me but in the process, making it look like he was working graveyard shifts when he was returning home with the mother of his child. As soon as I made a move, things took a turn for the worse. My ex-husband had me arrested by police, almost facing ten years in prison. Not to mention rape, verbal and physical abuse. I dealt with my car being vandalized my phone being in his possession, so I couldn't contact anybody about the abuse. The amount of cyberbullying that I endured was humiliating. I had fake social media pages created with images of me in the nude. He even had my photos placed on adult websites. When I finally made a move to escape. He was in custody with the police for a warrant with domestic violence. I return back home to start my life. It did not resume back to normal immediately. I became a victim of stalking. He was trying to kill me. He cut the brake lines off my car, vandalized my car, and stripped the tires. By the grace of God, a friend, a good Samaritan help me retrieve the vehicle and pay for the damages. That time was a very difficult time because he was still trying to control my life. Countless times he was making false calls to DCF for my children to be taken away.

Every day I lived my life in fear, which resulted in me having to live in a domestic violence shelter for maximum protection. Where I was residing, I was no longer able to reside there anymore because fear has taken over. In the process, my purpose was revealed. I decided to return to school in the midst of all my trials and tribulations. I went to school to become a licensed aesthetician and make-up artist. Throughout the course of time, I went through a series of things. I was arrested for a warrant pertaining to the case that I was facing ten years in prison. I was facing homelessness and so much more, but I knew God was carrying me. I always had the scripture embedded in my heart; "I can do all things through Christ who strengthens me" - Philippians 4:13.

Truthfully it took me going through all this pain to become what I was truly meant to be in life. All my life, I was told what I should be and kept following the advice of others. My life was in shambles and forced me to do what I always wanted to do. Rejection from domestic violence propelled me into my purpose. I had to go to a season of isolation to move in the direction that God needed me to be. I didn't understand it back then, but I completely understand it right now. In order to thrive, I had to heal my flesh. I had to crucify the very thing that wasn't of God in order to become what God had ordered for me. As mentioned in I Peter 5:7, "Cast all your anxiety on him because he cares for you." I had to fully rely on God. Every pain that I was feeling, including depression, I had to let it go and cast it on him." This was the beginning of me falling in love with Christ all over again. I had placed my heart in my trust more in a man than I did in Christ. The ending result was painful, and it nearly cost me my life. The purpose is often found after pain. Psalms 30:5 – "Weeping may endure for a night, but joy will come in the morning." My joy was coming. The joy of the Lord was getting ready to overtake me because I chose to walk in his will instead of mine. The decision to accept Christ means that you have to bear the cross. My cross was domestic violence. My flesh had to die in order for my spirit man tobe strengthened.

All I went through was to break generational curses in my household, within my family. There is always that one person in your family that is the sacrificial lamb. They are the designated person assigned to take the same beatings as Christ it. As time went by, I realize God chose me for this battle. What I endured was for the saving of many. I am grateful for this journey that I went through and who it has made me become. Romans 8:18 I consider that our present sufferings are not worth comparing with the glory that will be revealed in us. The scripture sums everything up. Everything that we go through is for the glory of God.

Every time I thought I was being rejected from something good, I was actually being redirectedto something better.~ Dr. Steve Maraboli

This deeply explains the meaning of rejection. I remember before my relationship with Christ, I considered rejection to be the most painful thing to occur in my life. But as I grew mature in Christ, I learned that rejection was his way of redirecting me in the right direction. Rejection is a detour that is forcing you to go back in the right way. Many of us have been rejected by something we loved and wanted so bad, and we thought it was the best thing for us. In the end, it resulted in heartbreak because it wasn't God's plan.

There is a quote by Tony Robbins that states, "Success is buried on the other side of rejection." It is the opportunity for you to make the correct selection. Rejection simply means that you will shine bright, and sometimes the light that shines brightly within you fuels people to reject you. They have to expel you because the glory that is in you cannot receive it. There are lessons learned in rejection. You learn to guard your heart, and in the process, humility becomesyour portion.

Many people fear rejection that stems from issues from their childhood. Some grew up in homes where they were neglected and rejected. Often they reflect on your past, which lingers into their current relationships. In most cases, it causes self-esteem. A quote from Harvey McKay says, "Most fears of rejection rest on the desire for approval from other people." Don't base your self-esteem on their opinions. People that seek approval are the ones who take rejection the hardest. Start speaking life into your spirit and replace all the negative emotions with positivity. Once you maintain a healthy relationship with God, it will allow you to strengthen your self-esteem. Maintain a circle that knows your value. Surround yourself with people who challenge you and remain honest with you. People who aren't openly honest with you and don't challenge you are the ones who make you susceptible to rejection. In order to receive the rejection, you have to be able to take direction.

Rejection doesn't disqualify you from the car. It simply qualifies you for the car. It's a form of protection. Protection intended for direction. Once we realize that rejection is a part of drawing us closer to God, we will begin to look at it as a way of God seeking us instead of punishing us. It is necessary, and it is a reminder to show us that we are in Christ, and we will endure his sufferings as long as we walk with him and believe in him. Christ didn't win the approval of man. He was continuously rejected for doing the will of the Lord. He was rejected by his own. He knows that he had to endure the very thing he went through for a purpose to be created. He wasn't rejected by strangers. He was rejected by those who are close to him. If we continue to seek God and read His word, we will always know that we are exempt from the same things that Christ in the world.

Ecclesiastes 1:9 - "There is nothing new under the sun." David was rejected because they thought he wasn't qualified. Leah was rejected and unloved. Jesus was rejected as the son of man. Job was suffering, and his friends advised him that he was the cause of all his trouble. That was a form of dismissal and abandonment. Every one of these characters went through a rejection that brought a blessing in the end.

What is God showing you IN your rejection season? What purpose does he have to draw out of you in your season of isolation? God's design for your life will come in the form of rejection. Romans 11:15, - "for if their rejection brought reconciliation to the world what will their acceptance be but life from the dead."

JOURNAL

Do you feel like you were rejected for a purpose? God often allows rejection to shape, mold and push you into your destiny. Write each season you felt you were rejected and how it has made you stonger today.

_____

_____

_____

_____

_____

_____

_____

_____

_____

_____

_____

_____

_____

_____

_____

_____

_____

CPSIA information can be obtained
at www.ICGtesting.com
Printed in the USA
BVHW091548260421
605865BV00012B/2678